THE PLANETS AND ME

ASTROLOGY FOR THE WILD CHILD

by Lady Samantha   illustrated by Jan Dolby

WILD CHILD SERIES

◆ FriesenPress

One Printers Way
Altona, MB R0G 0B0
Canada

www.friesenpress.com

Copyright © 2022 by Lady Samantha
First Edition — 2022

Additional Contributor
Jan Dolby, Illustrator

All rights reserved.

No part of this publication may be reproduced in any form, or by any means, electronic or mechanical, including photocopying, recording, or any information browsing, storage, or retrieval system, without permission in writing from FriesenPress.

ISBN
978-1-5255-9827-2 (Hardcover)
978-1-5255-9826-5 (Paperback)
978-1-5255-9828-9 (eBook)

1. JUVENILE NONFICTION, SCIENCE & NATURE, ASTRONOMY

Distributed to the trade by The Ingram Book Company

For my daughter Elora, who continues to inspire me. – L.S.

For my friend Lisa. – J.D.

SUN

I am the **SUN,** shining bright from my heart,
Claiming my right to be who I am.
I roar this truth with pride and love,
Expressing my life force wherever I can.

The Sun is my true self,
The strength of my pure creativity.
On the stage of life, I perform,
In spotlight for all to see.

MOON

My Moon is my heart's home,
Which resides deep within me.
Deep in this place,
I express my emotions safely.

MERCURY

Mercury is my **VOICE**,
How I speak and communicate,
How I listen to others,
And think about what it means to me.

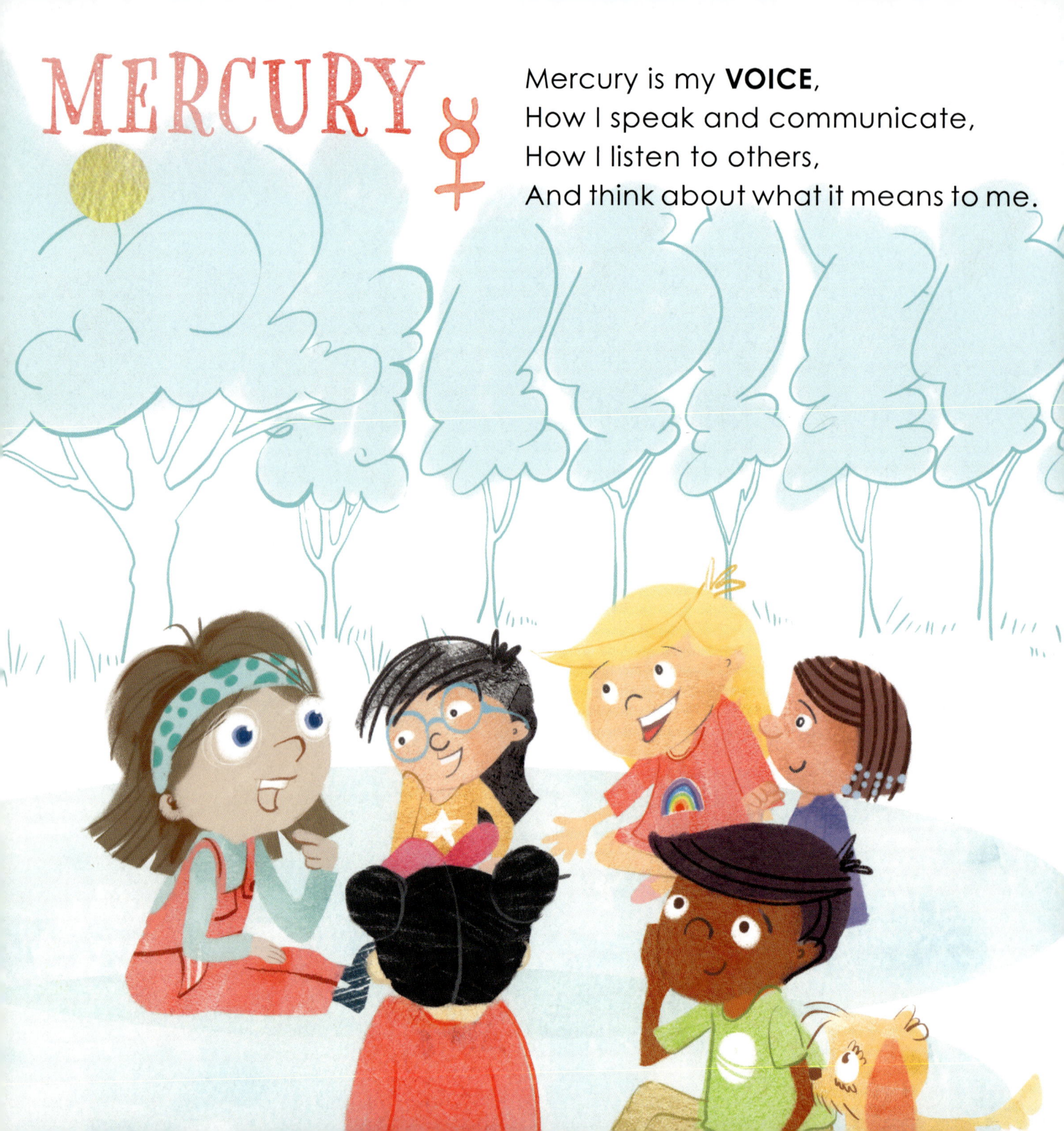

Mercury is my mind,
My opinions and my thoughts,
How I relate to information,
Based on what I am taught.

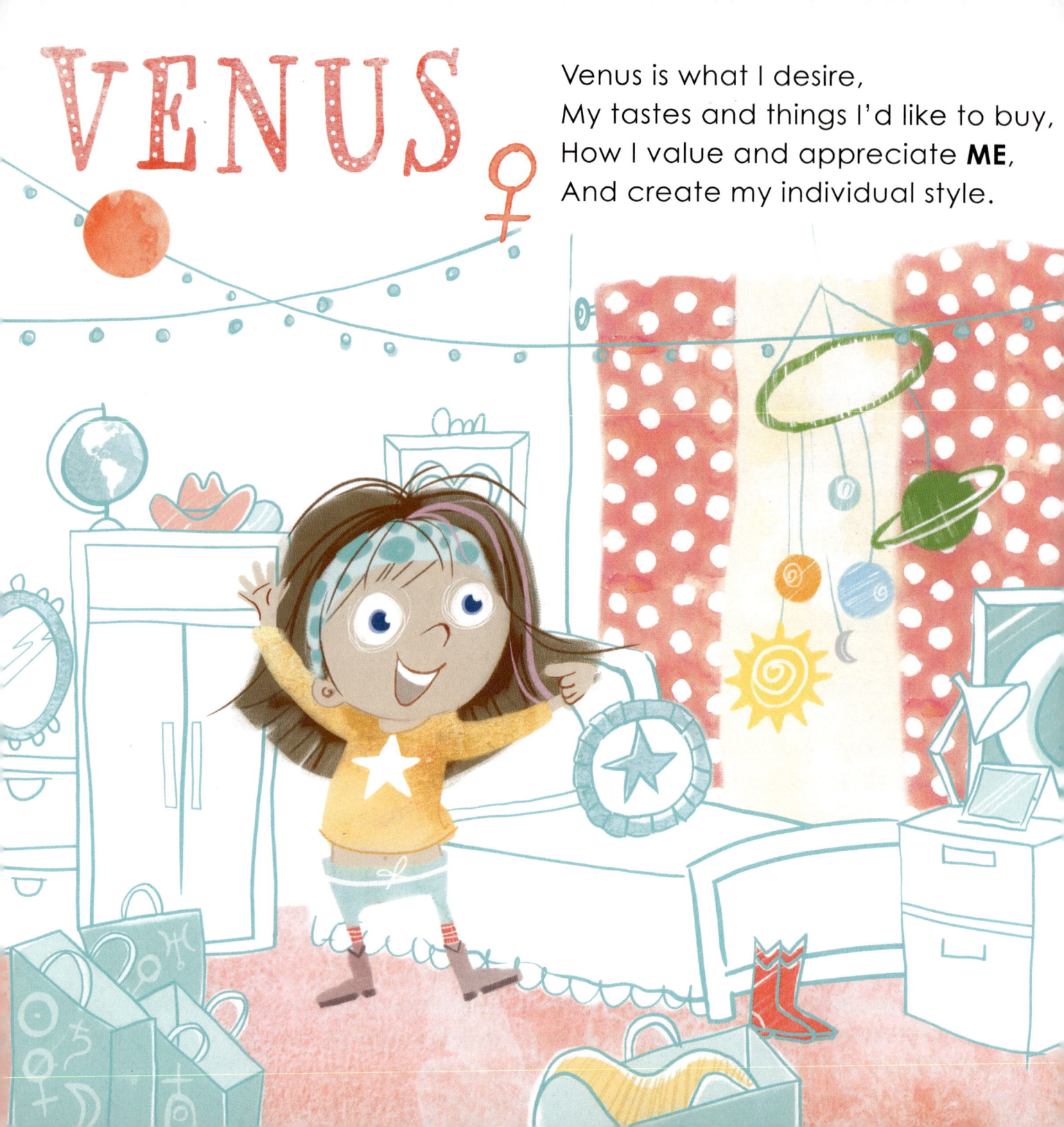

Venus teaches me about true beauty,
Accepting all of me, inside and out.
She shows me how to love others,
By first **LOVING** myself.

MARS ♂

I can do **ANYTHING!**
Mars makes me feel alive.
My courage in life,
My instincts to **THRIVE!**

Mars is how I take action,
Move my body and assert my **WILL**,
How I rise to battle,
With **WARRIOR SKILLS.**

LOVE is the only WAY

LOVE RULES

JUPITER ♃

The **BIGGEST** planet is Jupiter.
He teaches me how to grow,
How to expand,
   trust myself,
And be confident in what I know.

Jupiter shows me what I can become,
The **FUTURE ME** with goals and dreams,
A life of learning and wisdom,
Creating inspiring opportunities.

SATURN ♄

ugh!

Learning how to make choices,
From frustrations that arise in me,
Are Saturn's lessons of growing up,
Becoming **ALL** I can be.

Saturn is how I build,
Create with my own two hands,
Apply effort even when scared.
I CAN, I CAN, I CAN.

URANUS ♅

I AM SO EXCITED!

Nothing can hold me back!
I break the chains of boredom,
I invent!
I innovate!
I discover new facts!

Uranus is my special gift,
My unique mind that breaks the norm,
My need for higher purpose and change,
My goal to heal the world.

NEPTUNE ♆

I dreamt last night of a fairy,
The most beautiful of all.
Upon closer inspection, I realized
Her face was adorned with **LOVE**.

More **LOVE** than one could hold,
My heart never felt so **FREE**.
Everything that makes life feel magical,
That's Neptune's love in me.

PLUTO

Pluto is the big powerful **CHANGE**
When my world turns upside down.
Fears that lock me in
And pull me down into the ground.

Pluto is the intensity
I feel deep down inside,
Urging me to let go and transform my fear,
The place where **TRUE POWER RESIDES**.

♇ PLUTO

♆ NEPTUNE

URANUS ♅

MOON ☽

♄ SATURN

So these are the planets that live within me,
That support the star, the Sun.
The Sun, **ME**, is connected to **ALL**.
THE SUN, THE ALL, THE ONE.

FUN FACTS ABOUT PLANETS

The Sun is the star at the centre of our solar system, the Milky Way. All the planets orbit around the Sun. It supports life on Earth.

Mercury is the closest planet to the Sun. Therefore, if you look up into the sky on any given day, Mercury is never that far away from the Sun.

The Moon is the Earth's satellite. It orbits the Earth every 29.5 days. We experience this cycle through the changing faces of the Moon, from new to full and back to new.

Mars is called the red planet. Astronomers suggest that it is highly probable that Mars once sustained life because we can see the remnants of ocean beds and rivers on its dry surface.

Venus is a hot, fiery planet similar in size to the Earth but closer to the Sun. A day on Venus is 117 Earth days. It rotates very slowly.

Earth is our home. The distance between the Earth to the Sun, relative to the size of the Earth, creates the perfect equation for life on our planet.

Astrology is the study of the movement of the planets in relation to our experience on Earth. We experience the planets moving around us, so astrologers call the Sun and Moon planets. We understand this is not actually true and that the planets and Earth actually revolve around the Sun.

♃ **Jupiter** is the largest planet. It's so large that you could fit the Moon, Mercury, Earth, Venus, Mars, Saturn, Uranus, Neptune, and Pluto inside and still have more space!

♅ ♆ **Uranus** and **Neptune** were discovered only after the invention of the telescope. They are not visible with the naked eye. They are both considered ice giants and have very faint rings.

♄ **Saturn** is best known for its giant rings—eight rings in fact—that are made up of shattered moons, rock, ice, and debris.

♇ **Pluto** is now considered by astronomers to be a dwarf planet and part of an asteroid belt called the Kuiper Belt that orbits far out in the solar system beyond Neptune. It was discovered one hundred years ago.

LADY SAMANTHA is a professional astrologer from Toronto specializing in natal chart analysis, and relationship and parenting astrology. She is the vision behind The Rock Store Healing Centre and Moons of Avalon online portal for astrological education. When she is not teaching, writing, or working with clients, she can be found somewhere in nature with her horses, dogs, and family, while simultaneously staring up into the sky, questioning our connection to everything. Find out more at ladysamantha.com.

JAN DOLBY is an internationally published illustrator and character designer located in the Toronto area. She searches the nighttime sky for stars and planets at her Lake Huron summer cottage. You can see more of her work at jandolby.com.

Printed in Canada